This book belongs to:

Managing Editor
Mara Ellen Guckian

Editor in Chief
Brent L. Fox, M. Ed.

Creative Director
Sarah M. Fournier

Cover Artist
Kelly McMahon

Art Coordinator
Renée Mc Elwee

Illustrator
Kelly McMahon

Imaging
Amanda R. Harter

Publisher
Mary D. Smith, M.S. Ed.

Edupress
A Division of Teacher Created Resources
12621 Western Avenue
Garden Grove, CA 92841
www.teachercreated.com

ISBN: 978-1-4206-0164-0

Reprinted, 2025
Made in U.S.A.

A Division of Teacher Created Resources

Introduction

This is a book to help learn sight words 1–50. Sight words are important words we use every day. Each one must be memorized since sight words do not follow regular spelling rules. This book provides practice reading, tracing, writing, and spelling each important word.

How to Use Page 3

Page 3 is a checklist of the 50 sight words featured in this book. Check off each word as it is learned, or use the list after finishing the book to review the words.

How to Use Pages 4–28

There are two sight words featured on each page. First, trace each sight word to practice forming the letters correctly. Then, say each letter to spell the word that was traced. Finally, write each sight word.

How to Use Pages 29–32

It is time to practice using the sight words that have been learned. First, read the four sight words in the word boxes at the top of each page. Then, use each word to complete one of the sentences. There are pictures to help with other new words. Reread each sentence to check that the sight words were used correctly.

Have fun!

Sight Words Checklist

- [ ] the
- [ ] of
- [ ] and
- [ ] a
- [ ] to
- [ ] in
- [ ] is
- [ ] you
- [ ] that
- [ ] it

- [ ] he
- [ ] was
- [ ] for
- [ ] on
- [ ] are
- [ ] as
- [ ] with
- [ ] his
- [ ] they
- [ ] I

- [ ] at
- [ ] be
- [ ] this
- [ ] have
- [ ] from
- [ ] or
- [ ] one
- [ ] had
- [ ] by
- [ ] word

- [ ] but
- [ ] not
- [ ] what
- [ ] all
- [ ] were
- [ ] we
- [ ] when
- [ ] your
- [ ] can
- [ ] said

- [ ] there
- [ ] use
- [ ] an
- [ ] each
- [ ] which
- [ ] she
- [ ] do
- [ ] how
- [ ] their
- [ ] if

the

Trace it.

the

the

Write it.

of

Trace it.

of

of

Write it.

and

Trace it.

and

and

Write it.

a

Trace it.

a

a

Write it.

to

Trace it.

to

to

Write it.

in

Trace it.

in

in

Write it.

is

Trace it.

is

is

Write it.

you

Trace it.

you

you

Write it.

that

Trace it.

that

that

Write it.

it

Trace it.

it

it

Write it.

he

Trace it.

he

he

Write it.

was

Trace it.

was

was

Write it.

for

Trace it.

for

for

Write it.

on

Trace it.

on

on

Write it.

are

Trace it.

are

are

Write it.

as

Trace it.

as

as

Write it.

with

Trace it.

with

with

Write it.

his

Trace it.

his

his

Write it.

they

Trace it.

they

they

Write it.

I

Trace it.

I

I

Write it.

at

Trace it.

at

at

Write it.

be

Trace it.

be

be

Write it.

this

Trace it.

this

this

Write it.

have

Trace it.

have

have

Write it.

from

Trace it.

from

from

Write it.

or

Trace it.

or

or

Write it.

one

Trace it.

one

one

Write it.

had

Trace it.

had

had

Write it.

by

Trace it.

by

by

Write it.

word

Trace it.

word

word

Write it.

but

Trace it.

but

but

Write it.

not

Trace it.

not

not

Write it.

what

Trace it.

what

what

Write it.

all

Trace it.

all

all

Write it.

were

Trace it.

were

were

Write it.

we

Trace it.

we

we

Write it.

when

Trace it.

when

when

Write it.

your

Trace it.

your

your

Write it.

can

Trace it.

can

can

Write it.

said

Trace it.

said

said

Write it.

there

Trace it.

there

there

Write it.

use

Trace it.

use

use

Write it.

an

Trace it.

an

an

Write it.

each

Trace it.

each

each

Write it.

which

Trace it.

which

which

Write it.

she

Trace it.

she

she

Write it.

do

Trace it.

do

do

Write it.

how

Trace it.

how

how

Write it.

their

Trace it.

their

their

Write it.

if

Trace it.

if

if

Write it.

Use the words in the word bank to fill in the missing word in each sentence.

in	to	is	you

1. She wants ________  .
swim

2. Can ________ see the  ?
hen

3. This  ________ big.
dish

4. Put him ________ the  .
crib

Use the words in the word bank to fill in the missing word in each sentence.

it	that	he	was

1. I want ______  .

cup

2. Did ______ kick the  ?

ball

3. It ______ a big  .

jet

4. Put ______ on the  .

rug

Use the words in the word bank to fill in the missing word in each sentence.

at	be	this	have

1. I sit in the  tub ______  night.

2. Can we play ______  drum?

3. Do you ______ a  duck?

4. I want to ______ a  vet.

Use the words in the word box to fill in the missing word at the beginning of each sentence.

Which	She	Do	How

1. ________ you want to  ?

run

2. ________ do you win the  ?

game

3. ________  do you want?

doll

4. ________ will use the  .

mop